BEN MOO

Ode to a Nightingale

Poem by John Keats (1795–1821)

A cycle of eight songs
for baritone and piano

Commissioned by Suzie Kovner
for her husband Bruce Kovner
in commemoration of his 65th birthday.

On the cover: Cragsmoor Irises, oil on canvas (detail),
24 x 18 inches, by Ben Moore

First printing: July 2018

ED 4720

ISBN 978-1-5400-3145-7

G. SCHIRMER, Inc.

DISTRIBUTED BY

Copyright © 2018 by G. Schirmer, Inc.
International Copyright Secured All Rights Reserved

www.musicsalesclassical.com
www.halleonard.com

Contact Us:
Hal Leonard
7777 West Bluemound Road
Milwaukee, WI 53213
Email: info@halleonard.com

In Europe contact:
Hal Leonard Europe Limited
Distribution Centre, Newmarket Road
Bury St Edmunds, Suffolk, IP33 3YB
Email: info@halleonardeurope.com

In Australia contact:
Hal Leonard Australia Pty. Ltd.
4 Lentara Court
Cheltenham, Victoria, 3192 Australia
Email: info@halleonard.com.au

BEN MOORE

The music of American composer Ben Moore includes art song, opera, musical theatre, cabaret, chamber music, choral music, and comedy material. His work has been called "brilliant" and "gorgeously lyrical" by the *New York Times* while *Opera News* has praised the "easy tunefulness" and "romantic sweep" of his songs. Singers who have performed his work include Deborah Voigt, Susan Graham, Frederica von Stade, Isabel Leonard, Lawrence Brownlee, Robert White, Nathan Gunn, and Audra McDonald.

Ben's songs can be heard on Deborah Voigt's album *All My Heart* (EMI), Nathan Gunn's *Just Before Sunrise* (SonyBMG), Lawrence Brownlee's *This Heart that Flutters* (Opus Arte), and *Susan Graham at Carnegie Hall* (Warner Classics). *Dear Theo* (Delos records) features three of Ben's song cycles, including *Dear Theo*, based on the letters of Vincent van Gogh; *So Free Am I*, on poems by women; and *Ode to a Nightingale*.

Moore composed the scores for three operas including *Enemies, a Love Story* which premiered at Palm Beach Opera in 2015 and saw a second performance at Kentucky Opera in 2018. Based on the novel by Isaac Bashevis Singer, with a libretto by Nahma Sandrow, the opera has been called "an important new work that will find its place among those works that audiences will be moved by..." (Fred Plotkin/WQXR). *Odyssey* and *Robin Hood* are youth operas commissioned by the Glimmerglass Festival with librettos by Kelley Rourke. *Odyssey* premiered at Glimmerglass in 2015 and has since been seen at the Metropolitan Museum of Art and Minnesota Opera. Opera News called it "an opera for all ages" with an "ebullient and lyrical" score. The work returned to Glimmerglass in July 2018. *Robin Hood* premiered at Glimmerglass in August 2017, was seen at Seattle Opera in February 2018, and Houston Grand Opera in June 2018.

In 2006 the Metropolitan Opera featured two of his comedy songs in a gala broadcast nationally. 2006 also saw the release of the volume *Ben Moore: 14 Songs* published by G. Schirmer, Inc. Reviewing the album, *Classical Singer Magazine* wrote: ". . . you can find a breath of fresh air in the settings included in this volume... This composer is not afraid of the past, but rather embraces many of the most beautiful aspects of his artistic heritage while imbuing his work with its own personal colors and tones."

Born on January 2, 1960, in Syracuse, New York, Moore grew up in Clinton, New York and graduated from Hamilton College. Ben is also a painter with an MFA from The Parsons School of Design.

CONTENTS

ODE TO A NIGHTINGALE
by John Keats

My heart aches, and a drowsy numbness pains
 My sense, as though of hemlock I had drunk,
Or emptied some dull opiate to the drains
 One minute past, and Lethe-wards had sunk:
'Tis not through envy of thy happy lot,
 But being too happy in thine happiness,—
  That thou, light-winged Dryad of the trees,
   In some melodious plot
 Of beechen green, and shadows numberless,
  Singest of summer in full-throated ease.

O, for a draught of vintage! that hath been
 Cool'd a long age in the deep-delved earth,
Tasting of Flora and the country green,
 Dance, and Provençal song, and sunburnt mirth!
O for a beaker full of the warm South,
 Full of the true, the blushful Hippocrene,
  With beaded bubbles winking at the brim,
   And purple-stained mouth;
 That I might drink, and leave the world unseen,
  And with thee fade away into the forest dim:

Fade far away, dissolve, and quite forget
 What thou among the leaves hast never known,
The weariness, the fever, and the fret
 Here, where men sit and hear each other groan;
Where palsy shakes a few, sad, last gray hairs,
 Where youth grows pale, and spectre-thin, and dies;
  Where but to think is to be full of sorrow
   And leaden-eyed despairs,
 Where Beauty cannot keep her lustrous eyes,
  Or new Love pine at them beyond to-morrow.

Away! away! for I will fly to thee,
 Not charioted by Bacchus and his pards,
But on the viewless wings of Poesy,
 Though the dull brain perplexes and retards:
Already with thee! tender is the night,
 And haply the Queen-Moon is on her throne,
  Cluster'd around by all her starry Fays;
   But here there is no light,
 Save what from heaven is with the breezes blown
  Through verdurous glooms and winding mossy ways.

I cannot see what flowers are at my feet,
        Nor what soft incense hangs upon the boughs,
But, in embalmed darkness, guess each sweet
        Wherewith the seasonable month endows
The grass, the thicket, and the fruit-tree wild;
        White hawthorn, and the pastoral eglantine;
                Fast fading violets cover'd up in leaves;
                        And mid-May's eldest child,
        The coming musk-rose, full of dewy wine,
                The murmurous haunt of flies on summer eves.

Darkling I listen; and, for many a time
        I have been half in love with easeful Death,
Call'd him soft names in many a mused rhyme,
        To take into the air my quiet breath;
                Now more than ever seems it rich to die,
        To cease upon the midnight with no pain,
                While thou art pouring forth thy soul abroad
                        In such an ecstasy!
        Still wouldst thou sing, and I have ears in vain—
                To thy high requiem become a sod.

Thou wast not born for death, immortal Bird!
        No hungry generations tread thee down;
The voice I hear this passing night was heard
        In ancient days by emperor and clown:
Perhaps the self-same song that found a path
        Through the sad heart of Ruth, when, sick for home,
                She stood in tears amid the alien corn;
                        The same that oft-times hath
        Charm'd magic casements, opening on the foam
                Of perilous seas, in faery lands forlorn.

Forlorn! the very word is like a bell
        To toll me back from thee to my sole self!
Adieu! the fancy cannot cheat so well
        As she is fam'd to do, deceiving elf.
Adieu! adieu! thy plaintive anthem fades
        Past the near meadows, over the still stream,
                Up the hill-side; and now 'tis buried deep
                        In the next valley-glades:
        Was it a vision, or a waking dream?
                Fled is that music:—Do I wake or sleep?

BEN MOORE
Ode to a Nightingale

For Bruce Kovner

ODE TO A NIGHTINGALE

I. My heart aches

Poem by
John Keats

Music by
Ben Moore

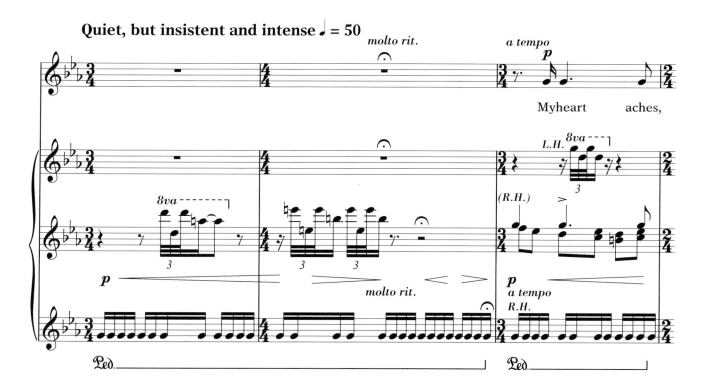

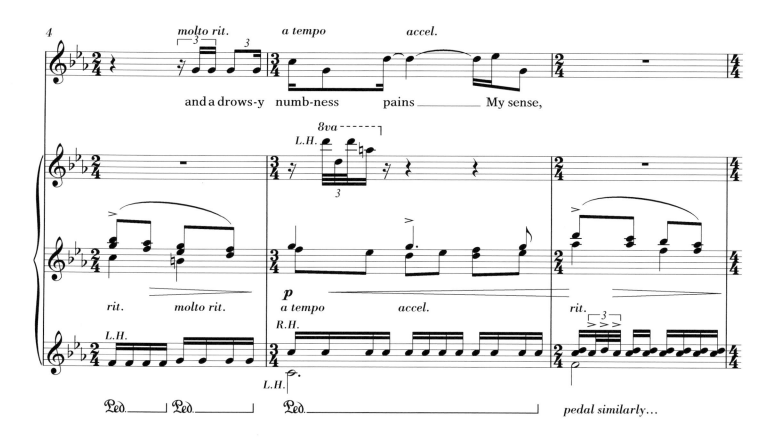

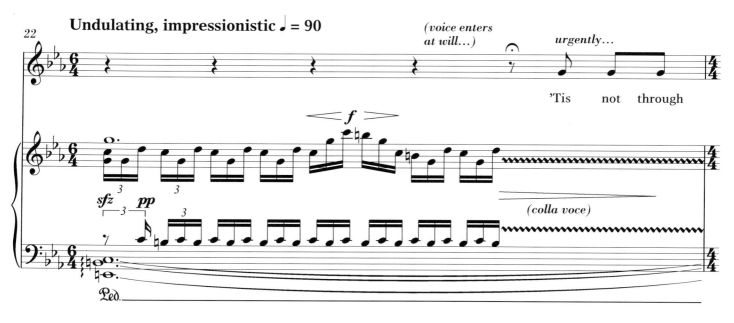

Undulating, impressionistic ♩ = 90

(voice enters at will…)   *urgently…*

'Tis   not   through

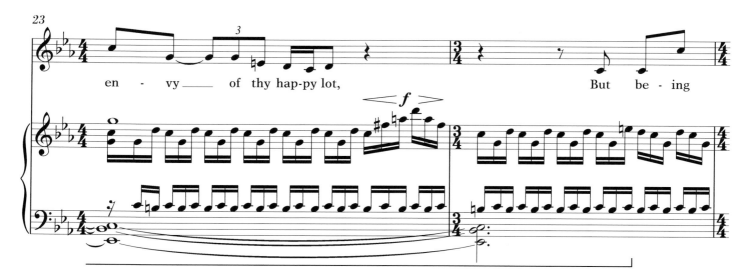

en - vy ___ of thy hap-py lot,   But be - ing

too hap - py in thine hap - pi - ness, That thou, —

light - wing - ed Dry - ad ___ of the trees, In

some mel - o - di - ous plot Of

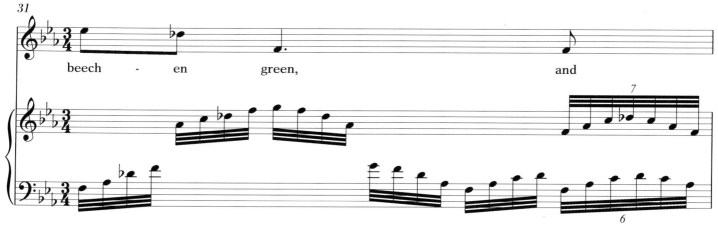

beech - en green, and

shad - ows num - ber - less,

Ad Lib., impressionistic…

♩ = 80

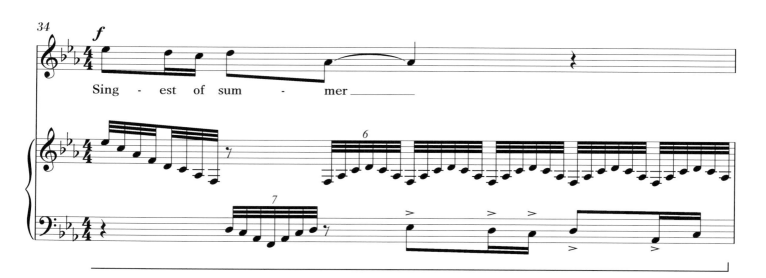

Sing - est of sum - mer

Sing - est of sum - mer

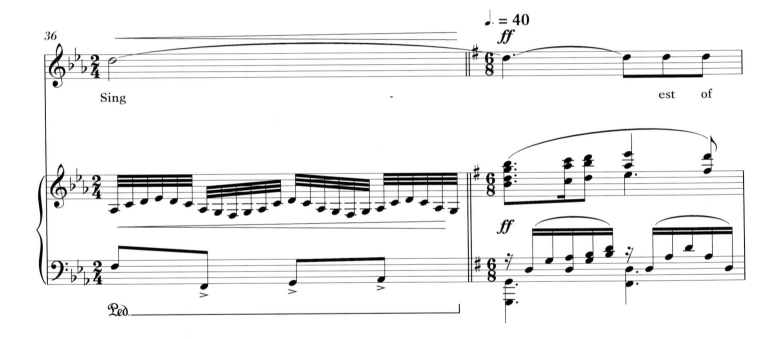

♩. = 40

ff

Sing - est of

ff

sum - mer in full - throat - ed

sf *pp*

ease _____ Sing - est, of sum - mer _____

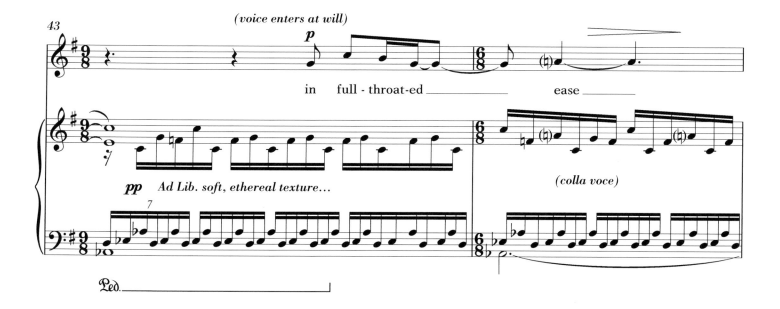

(voice enters at will)

in full - throat-ed _____ ease _____

pp Ad Lib. soft, ethereal texture…

(colla voce)

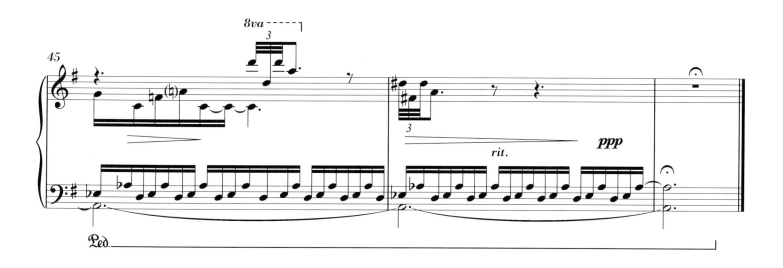

II. O, for a draught

Rubato, with earthiness and drive ♩ = 90

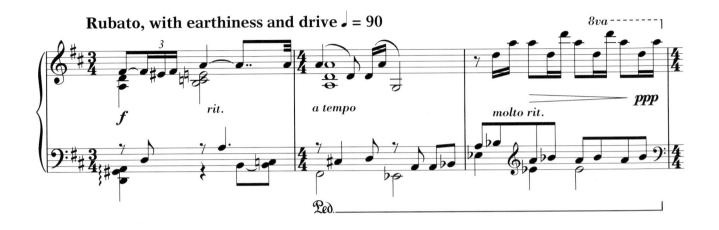

O, ___ for a draught of vin-tage! ___ that hath been Cool'd ___ a long

age in the deep del - ved earth, Tast-ing of Flor-a

and the coun try green, _____ Dance and Pro-ven-çal

song, and sun - burnt mirth! _____

O for a beak-er full of the

warm South _ Full of the true, the blush-ful Hip-po-crene, With bead-ed bub-bles

wink-ing at the brim, And pur-ple stain-ed mouth;

light pedal...

Fast

III. Fade far away

pedal similarly…

Fade _____ far _____ a-way, _____ dis-

solve, and quite for-get What thou a-mong the leaves _____

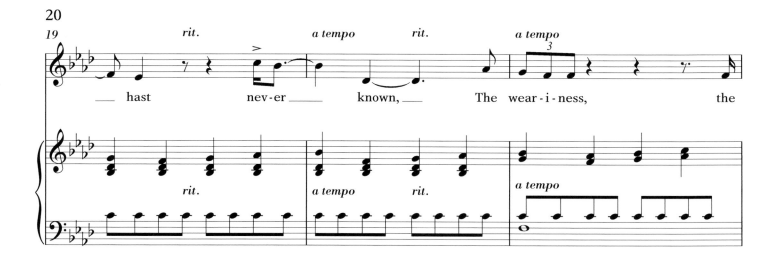

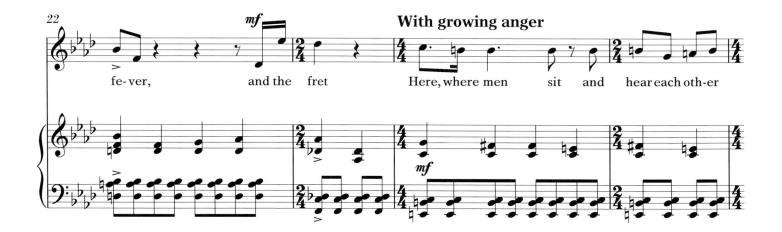

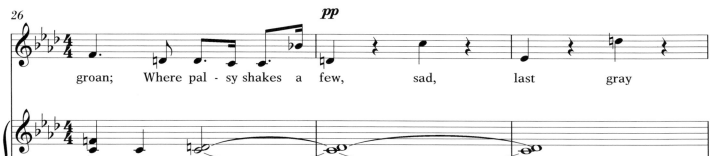

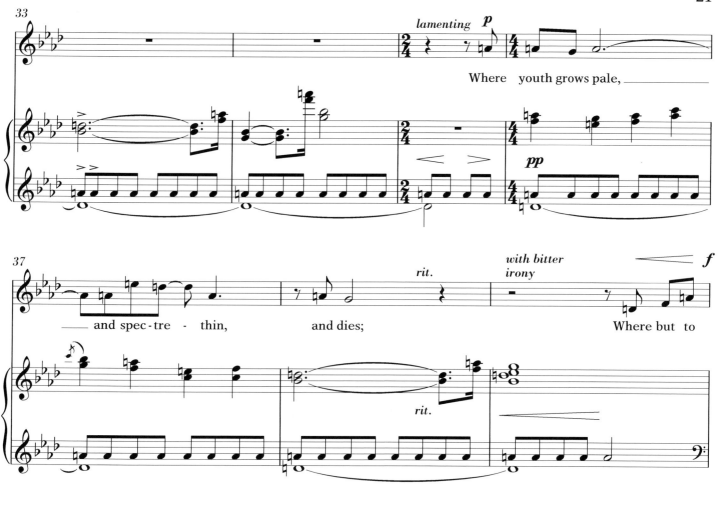

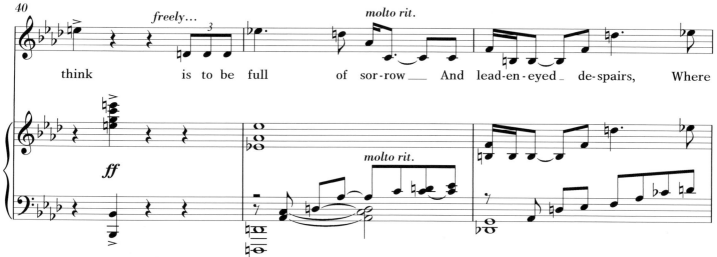

Or new Love pine _____ at them be-yond to-mor-row. __

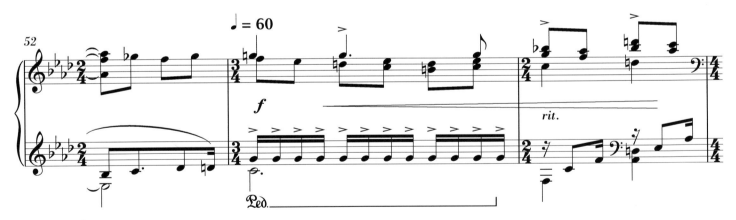

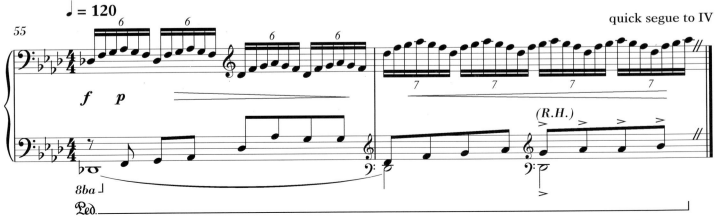

quick segue to IV

IV. Away! away!

light, Save what from hea-ven is with the bree - zes blown

Through ver - dur-ous glooms and wind-ing mos-sy __ ways.

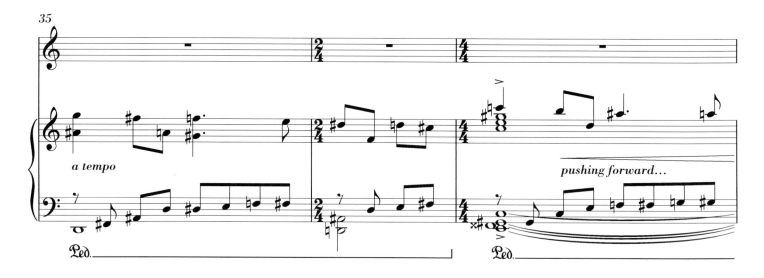

a tempo

pushing forward...

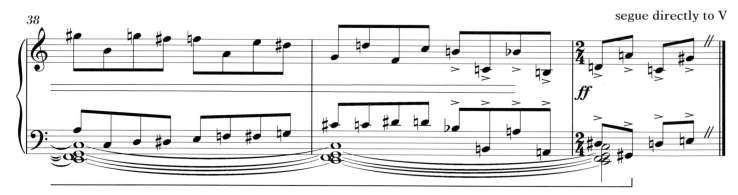

segue directly to V

V. I cannot see what flowers

Delicate, impressionistic, undulating tempo ♩ = around 110

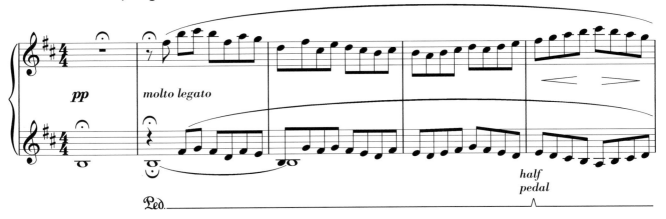

Nor what soft in-cense hangs

up - on the boughs,

But, in em-balm - ed dark - ness, guess each sweet

Where - with the sea - son-a-ble month en-

dows The grass, the thick-et, and the fruit - tree

wild; White haw-thorn, and the pas - tor-al eg - lan-tine;

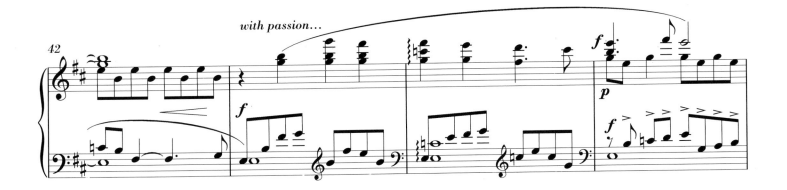

Fast fad-ing vio-lets cov-er'd up in leaves and

mid-May's eld - est child The com-ing musk rose, full of dew-y wine

The mur-mur-ous haunt of flies on sum-mer eves. __

VI. Darkling I listen*

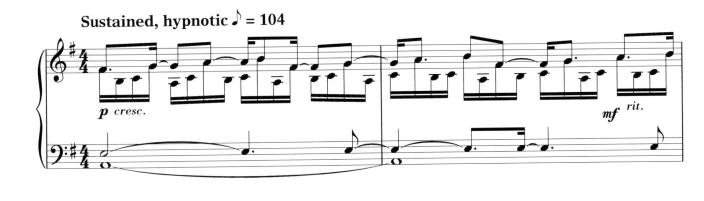

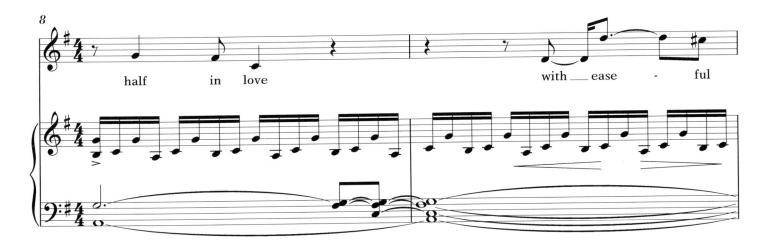

Death, _____ Call'd him soft _____

_____ names in man-y a _____ mus - èd _____ rhyme, _____ To

take in - to the air my _____ qui - et _

_____ breath; _____ Now _____ more than

ev - er _____ seems it   seems it

rich   to die,   To cease up - on the

mid - night   with   no   pain,

While thou art pour - ing _ forth thy

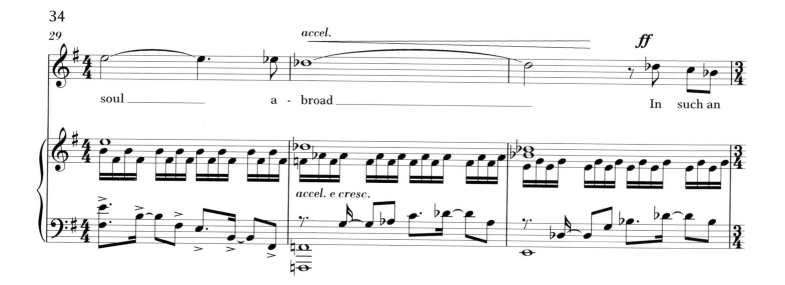

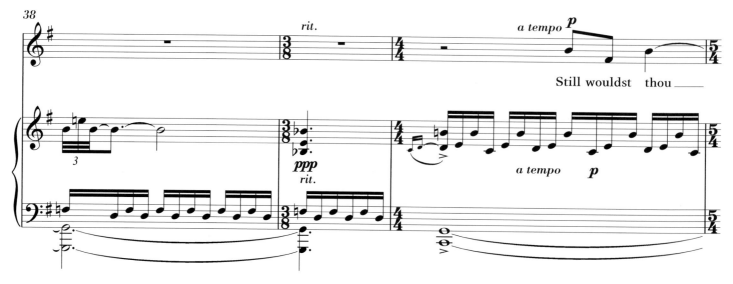

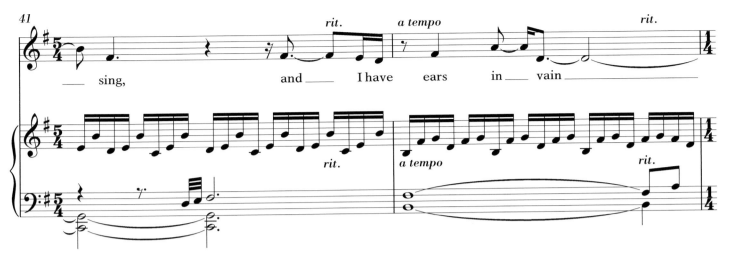

sing, and I have ears in vain

To thy high re - qui-em be-come a

sod.

VII. Thou wast not born for death

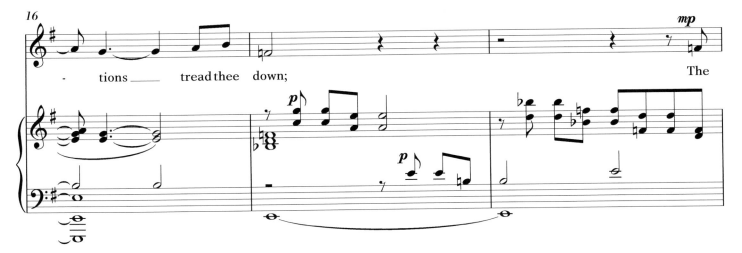

Slower, freely

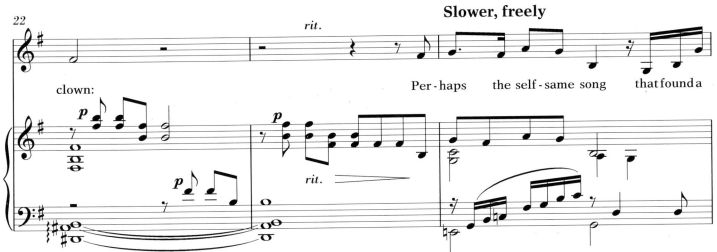

path Through the sad heart of Ruth, when, sick for home, She stood in tears a-

mid the a - lien corn;

the same _____ song ___

the same ___

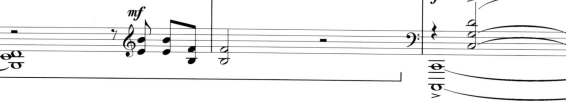

Expansive, Huge...

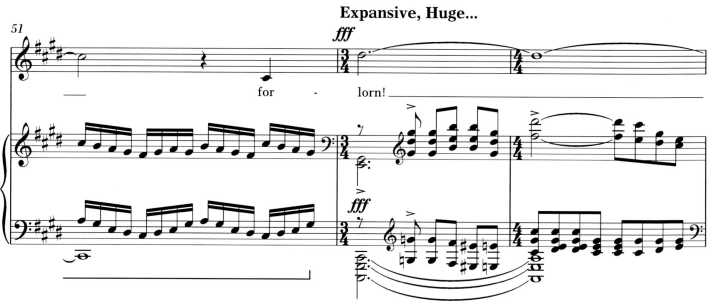

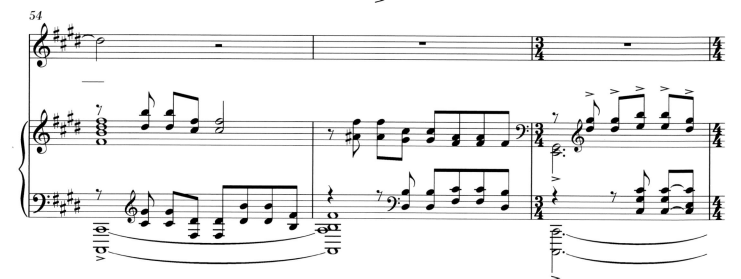

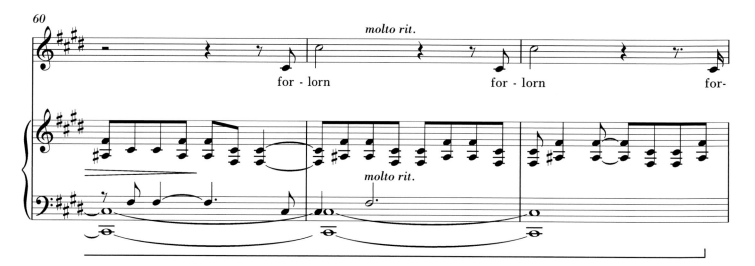

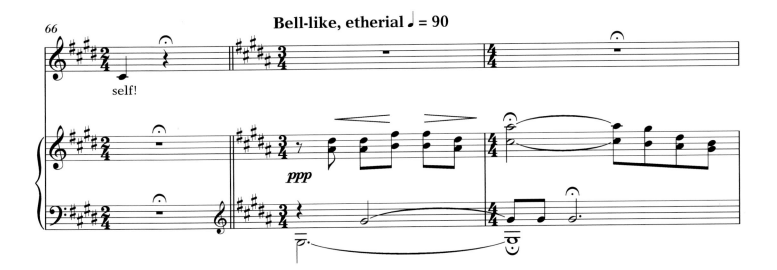

VIII. Adieu!

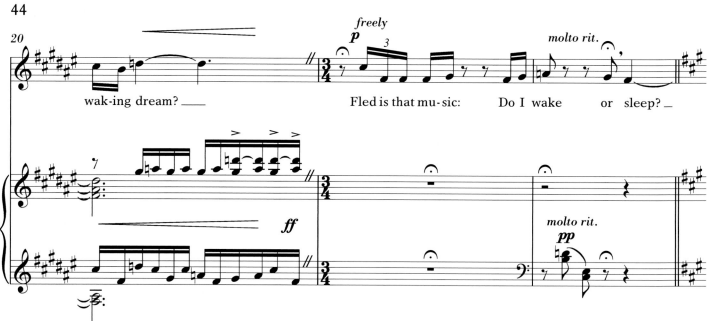

wak-ing dream? _____   Fled is that mu-sic: Do I wake   or sleep? _

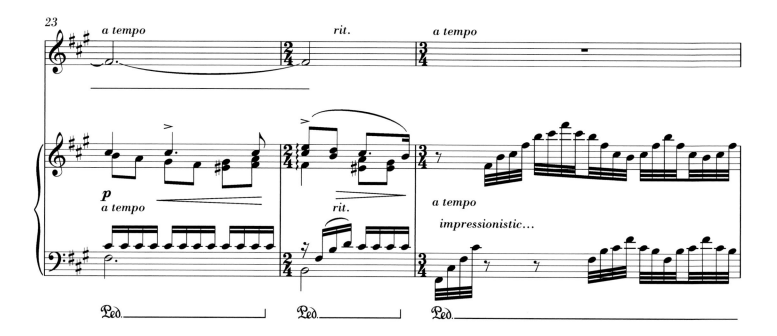

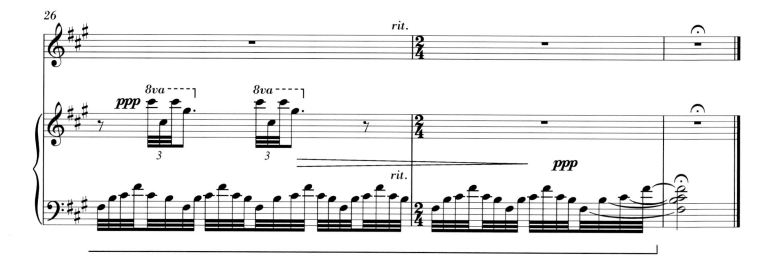